Sermons On The
Be-Attitudes

Invitations To The
Kingdom Of Heaven

John A. Terry

CSS Publishing Company, Inc., Lima, Ohio

SERMONS ON THE BE-ATTITUDES

Some scripture quotations are from the *Revised Standard Version of the Bible*, copyrighted 1946, 1952, ©, 1971, 1973, by the Division of Christian Education of the National Council of the Churches of Christ in the USA. Used by permission.

Some scripture quotations are from the *Good News Bible*, in Today's English Version. Copyright © American Bible Society, 1966, 1971, 1976. Used by permission.

Some scripture quotations are from the *King James Version of the Bible*, in the public domain.

Library of Congress Cataloging-in-Publication Data

Terry, John, 1943-
    Sermons on the Be-attitudes : invitations to the kingdom of heaven / John A. Terry.
        p.   cm.
    ISBN 0-7880-0764-5
    1. Beatitudes—Sermons. 2. Congregational churches—Sermons. 3. Sermons—American. I. Title.
BT382.T47   1997
241.5'3—dc20   96-38666
                                                                                CIP

This book is available in the following formats, listed by ISBN:
    0-7880-0764-5   Book
    0-7880-0883-8   Mac
    0-7880-0884-6   IBM 3 1/2
    0-7880-0885-5   Sermon Prep

PRINTED IN U.S.A.

To Chuck,
Eli and
all our children

Table Of Contents

Preface

For as many years as I can remember I have preached from the lectionary. Normally I spend a good part of my summer planning services and sermons for the coming year. But sometimes events happen which change these plans. A few days before Christmas 1992, my wife announced to me that she was with child. We were both astonished and delighted. At that time we had been married for sixteen years and, based on all medical evidence, we were not able to conceive and bear children. Choosing adoption, we were blessed with two wonderful sons. That was the number of children we wanted, and another child was a surprise and a blessing, a gift from a grace-giving God.

But that following March, in the eighteenth week of pregnancy, we suffered a miscarriage, accompanied by medical complications which nearly cost my wife her life.

After a brief leave of absence, I returned to preaching for the rest of the Lenten season. After Easter I felt a compulsion to deviate from my preaching plans made during the summer, and decided to do a series of sermons on the Beatitudes. I did not know what was leading me to do this, except that it seemed like the right thing to do.

It turned out to be therapeutic for me as I wrestled with the meaning of the Beatitudes in our time. As I look back, I have come to understand that, given the loss we suffered, I needed to reconsider the events of my life in the light of the Beatitudes. In popular religion, "blessings" refer to what you get — dollars, position, family, friends, and health. But what appeared to be the blessing of another child was given and taken away. As I worked through these sermons I was reminded that in biblical religion blessings come through both what is given and what is denied, in both joy and sorrow.

But the blessings of God are not simply what we get for ourselves, but how each experience, each loss or gain, brings us closer to God.

It is hard for me to believe that God decides babies should die or we experience any other such sorrow, but I believe that the God who tests us through these trials gives gifts of the spirit to those who face the trials with faith in Christ. I hope that by the grace of God these sermons may prove helpful to others.

1

The Poor In Spirit

Matthew 5:1-12

When Jesus spoke these words, he had sat down with his disciples. These are not generic "words to live by" that get published in the Sunday magazine section. These are words Jesus spoke particularly to the disciples. That is why they went up the mountain to be alone.

The word translated as "blessed" is commonly translated today as "happy." Robert Schuller wrote a book titled *The Be Happy Attitudes*. There is a joy the word implies. The problem with the word "happy" is that it is rooted in the old English word "hap" which means chance. These are not things that occur by chance. They are part of the structure of the Kingdom of God.

A number of years ago the cartoonist Charles Schulz, creator of the *Peanuts* cartoon strip, produced a series of books under the title *Happiness Is ...*, including *Happiness Is ... A Warm Puppy*. The problem with calling these the "be happy attitudes" is that true and lasting happiness is not something outside of us, something we can acquire like a warm puppy.

These beatitudes are counted among the words of Jesus that turned upside down the values of common social order. Many see here the summary of Jesus' ethical teachings, yet it is more than a collection of commandments. These beatitudes are not a "to do" list. These beatitudes are not rules. These are not moral laws. When Jesus spoke these words, he spoke to a people for whom religion had, in large measure, been reduced to a series of rules. These are eschatological promises; that is, promises that will be fulfilled in God's time. They contrast our immediate reaction to present events, and God's final actions.

9

They are, in the words of Martin Luther King, about the content of our character. They do not simply point to what we do, but who we are to be. These are not the "do-attitudes," but the "be-attitudes." And they are attitudes, not rules.

But they are more than attitudes. They are conditions of living, a state of being, an expression of our relationship to God and our lives. Lasting happiness is discovered in our awareness of God in our lives, our openness to God, and our acknowledgment of our dependence on God. Here Jesus invites us into a new relationship with God.

The first of these beatitudes is: "Blessed are the poor in spirit, for theirs is the kingdom of heaven." More common advice today is expressed in *Ruddigore*, a Gilbert and Sullivan opera:

> *If you wish in the world to advance*
> *Your merits you're bound to enhance*
> *You must stir it and stump it,*
> *And blow your own trumpet,*
> *Or, trust me, you won't have a chance!*

The opposite of the poor in spirit are the proud in spirit. There is the pride of Peter who, blowing his own trumpet, said to Jesus, "Though they all fall away because of you, I will never fall away." He thought himself rich in his own power and determination. Soon Jesus was arrested and Peter began to follow Jesus at a distance, hanging back. When a woman said to him, "You were with Jesus, the Galilean," Peter, Mr. I-will-never-fall-away, said, "I do not know what you mean." When asked a second and third time, he said, "I do not know the man." Thinking himself wealthy in personal strength, he had no strength when it was needed. Better the faith of the hymn which says, "When other helpers fail, and comforts flee, help of the helpless, O abide with me."

In contrast to the poor in spirit are the proud in spirit. In classical Christian theology, pride is the chief sin. There is the account in *The Divine Comedy* of Virgil and Dante meeting the Angel of Humility. The angel struck Dante's forehead with his wings, and thus erased the pride-mark, while angel choirs sang, "Beati

10

pauperers spiritu." After that, Dante walked with light step because when the pride-mark is erased, all the other sins become a smaller burden.[1]

In contrast to striving after God's kingdom, which is the promise of this beatitude, is personal striving. There was a time when Christians believed that joy was putting Jesus first, others second and yourself last. However, in our time, the order has been reversed, putting self first, others second, and God last.

In the cartoon strip *Cathy*, there was a conversation between Cathy and Andrea. Cathy said, "When I was little, I put my own needs first and everyone said I was being selfish and inconsiderate. Now everyone says I'm SUPPOSED to put my own needs first." Andrea answered, "That's right, Cathy. Putting your own needs first is one of the most important things you can do to maintain your self-respect." Cathy looked sad when she asked, "How can I have any self-respect if I'm being selfish and inconsiderate?"

The poor in spirit are not the poor spirited, folks without vigor and force in their lives. Being "poor in spirit" is not being weak in spirit, but, having an attitude of faith which looks to God alone to preserve us in the midst of affliction. It is an awareness that we do not live by our own strength or ability, but by trusting in God. It is as the psalmist (34:6) said, "This poor man cried, and the Lord heard him, and saved him out of all his troubles." It is not those proud of themselves and their accomplishments who will inherit the kingdom, but those who rely on God.

To be poor in spirit, we empty ourselves of all desire to exercise self-will. We let go of preconceived ideas of God's will and way. To be poor in spirit, we discard ideas of our own goodness and spiritual self-sufficiency, or any other thing that stands between us and God. This is entrance into a life where God eliminates the need and pressure for seeking and gaining fame and fortune.

To be poor in spirit frees us from the error of the rich young ruler who came to Jesus for help, but "turned away sorrowful because he had great possessions." The tragedy came not because he was wealthy. Wealth is ethically neutral. It was tragic because he was enslaved by the love of money.

11

Instead of the way of the world which glorifies the lifestyles of the rich and famous, God singles out the ones who feel like losers, and showers grace upon them. Christ came to lift up the lowly, to claim them as God's beloved children and to transform them into God's faithful servants.

The poor in spirit have a teachable spirit. They are receptive people who know they need God's help and are ready to receive the help God gives. They know their own insufficiency. Some refer to this as humility. It is humility like the humus, like the earth, the down-to-earth folks who know who they are and who they are not.

The most difficult people for Jesus were those who considered themselves self-sufficient because they thought they were so good. It was the Pharisee who, comparing himself to another, bragged to God, "I am not like these other people." These are the ones with whom Jesus had trouble. Jesus' hero was the publican crying, "God be merciful to me, a sinner." It is this one poor in spirit who was first to receive Jesus' blessing.

The poor in spirit are not necessarily the economically poor. Poverty itself is not a virtue any more than wealth is a curse. This is not a promise that if you have had a rotten time in this life, you are promised something better later.

More is implied here than economic poverty. This poverty involves our need for God. It is an attitude of simplicity and dependence on God. Here being "poor" means to be without haughtiness, without pride of possession or place. Economic poverty can make us acutely aware of our need, just as wealth can be a terrible barrier. True blessing, true happiness, is not external — growing rich in dollars — but internal in the presence of God's kingdom.

This blessing is an invitation to honesty. Last year there was a sizable meeting of area clergy at Memorial Hospital. Dr. Jim Squires led the discussion. In the exercise he took us through, we discovered that the one thing about which more pastors felt most badly was their own spiritual life. Through the process of this conversation, the great majority of clergy present said that they felt their spiritual lives were inadequate. In one sense, it is troublesome to think of spiritual leaders who feel spiritually inadequate. But being able to admit you are poor in spirit is a blessing.

Billy Graham's biographer notes the quality of a "continuing sense of inadequacy" and dependence on God as a key to Graham's success. Billy once said, "The Lord had always arranged my life so that I have had to keep dependent on Him. Over and over again I went to my knees and asked the Spirit of Wisdom for guidance and direction. There were times I was tempted to flee from problems and pressures and my inability to cope with them; but somehow, even in moments of confusion and indecision, it seemed I could trace the steady hand of God's leading me on." [2]

"Blessed are the poor in spirit, for theirs is the kingdom of heaven." We all know these words. We could all probably say something about what they mean. I believe, however, there is a lot of doubt about these words. We don't doubt Jesus said them. We don't doubt that they ought to be true. But we may doubt that they really work. The way it seems to work is, "Blessed are the rich, for theirs is the kingdom on earth."

This is a blessing for those who depend on God at all important times, who keep intact their own moral purity, who know that however much they are victims of injustice, they will ultimately be vindicated and rewarded by God. In Maya Angelou's autobiography, *I Know Why the Caged Bird Sings*, she describes the effect of a revival service on a gathering of black worshipers. The preacher extolled the virtues of "charity," called on the believers to forgive their enemies, and encouraged them "to bear up under this life of toil and care, because a blessed home awaited them in the far-off bye and bye." The congregation felt consoled.

"They basked," Ms. Angelou wrote, "in the righteousness of the poor and the exclusiveness of the downtrodden." They believed what the preacher and the Bible said. The ugliness of their present lives would make little difference in the long run. They would finally overcome by the power of God.

The people in the revival tent seemed to have heard the consolation of the beatitudes. "You are blessed," Jesus said. But a few minutes later they experienced something else. Shortly after they left the tent, the worshipers were assailed by the sounds of honky-tonk music and stamping feet. Saturday night customers swelled Miss Grace's Barrelhouse. The night was filled with lights and noise and blues.

As the worshipers passed Miss Grace's Barrelhouse, their consolation ebbed. Suddenly they saw the reality of their situation. Regardless of the words of the preacher and the teachings of Jesus, they were society's outcasts. The blessings about which they were just taught merged with the cry, "How long, merciful Father? How long?" They were facing the collision between what is and the promise of what is to come.

Those listening may not have felt very blessed. The lives of those listening provided little evidence of what anyone would call good fortune. But the blessing was not because of the poverty or oppression they experienced, but because of the esteem in which God held them. It is not because of any privilege they had in this life, but because of the future God had for them.

We are not commanded to become poor, to mourn, to become meek, hungry and thirsty, but by God's grace these states of human experience are transformed so that the poor in spirit inherit the kingdom of God. God is the gracious giver and we are the humble receivers. The poor cannot afford to buy a kingdom. But in God's economy, the kingdom becomes theirs. These are not things we do to buy God's favor. But having nothing ourselves, God gives the ultimate gift.

In this blessing, the inheritance is the kingdom of heaven. Charles Allen (in *God's Psychiatry*) tells the story of Frederick William IV of Prussia visiting a school and asking the children some questions. Pointing to the stone in his ring, the flower in his buttonhole, and a bird that flew past the window, he asked to which kingdom each of them belonged. The children gave him the right answers: the mineral, the vegetable, and the animal kingdoms. Then he asked, "To what kingdom do I belong?" The beatitudes are all promises about the true kingdom to which we belong.

The beatitudes are descriptions of those who will receive the promises of the kingdom. The blessed are the agents through whom the kingdom of God becomes visible in our world. They are people not yet perfect, but converted, people headed in the direction of God's kingdom. We value God's Kingdom as the supreme good. These are not commandments but invitations to be accepted. These are not goals to be strived for, but ways we are to relate to God's present and coming kingdom. Jesus is not trying to show us all the things we are doing wrong, but inviting us into the kingdom.

"How blessed are those who know their need of God." (NEB)

"Fortunate are the humble in spirit, for theirs is the Kingdom of Heaven." (Anchor)

"Happy are those who are humble, who are not overconcerned with their importance, for they have God's approval."

"Happy are those who realize their spiritual poverty: they have already entered the kingdom of Reality."

"Blessed are the poor in spirit, for theirs is the kingdom of heaven." (RSV)

---

1. Dante, *The Divine Comedy*, "Purgatory," Canto XII.

2. John Pollock, *To All The Nation* (Harper and Row).

2

Those Who Mourn

Isaiah 40:1-5
Matthew 5:1-12

I believe we have developed a greater understanding of the meaning and means of mourning. In 1969, Elizabeth Kubler-Ross published her classic book titled *On Death and Dying*. In it she identified five basic stages in the grieving process: denial, anger, bargaining, depression, and acceptance. Personally and professionally, I have found these helpful categories in recognizing where I am in my grieving and where others are in theirs. I have also found it to be true that getting stuck in any one of the first four stages of denial, anger, bargaining, or depression keeps us from receiving the promised comfort.

These are valid categories in describing responses to a wide range of losses. When we were in Atlanta, there were several church members who, in a short period of time, suffered the loss of a parent through death. We decided that it would be helpful for us to gather all those interested and talk about loss, mourning, and grief. We met over a series of Sunday nights. I thought we would be talking just about loss through death.

However, we ended up discussing a great variety of losses. Some in the group were grieving a loss because of a death. Others were grieving because they had lost a job. Others grieved over having to leave their hometown. Others were grieving over shattered family relationships. One mourned the loss of physical well-being.

As we took turns examining those things over which people were grieving, we found that the way in which people were mourning these various losses was strikingly similar, basically following the patterns observed by Elizabeth Kubler-Ross.

It is good that our society has moved away from the notion that the way to deal with a loss is to keep a stiff upper lip. It is good that there is a lot more openness in many places about loss and grief. But there is still much work to do.

Some seem to cling to their grief as a way to call attention to themselves and to create sympathy. Others confuse mourning with simply being depressed. Still others are simply pessimists who see only the negative side of things. Mourning itself is not necessarily a virtue. Many criminals mourn having gotten caught. Nor does this mean that being sad is the only way to be Christian.

Our society has not fully matured in our capacity to mourn. There seem to be fewer mourners at funerals. In the time of my ministry I have seen a move from two days of calling hours at funeral homes to a single day and, often, no calling hours at all.

In fact, many would say, "Happy are the hard-boiled, for they never let life hurt them." Stoic philosophers would say, "Do not mourn. Self-control is a better answer than sorrow." It does seem that for many folks insulating themselves from their feelings and the pain of others is their way of life. Many seem content being hollow people living without the compassion of Christ. There are people who, as St. Paul identified as the callous, are unable to feel another's pain (Ephesians 4:19). They must be pitied, for they will never know this blessing.

The popular blessing sought today is not mourning but "peace of mind." Saying "Happy are the sad" appears to be an oxymoron, a nonsense statement. In contrast to those who say, "Go, enjoy," Jesus says, "Go, mourn." In contrast to our instinct to avoid pain, Jesus is telling us to face it.

You may have heard of Father Damien who for thirteen years was a missionary to the lepers on Molokai. In time, he too contracted the dreaded disease. He learned of it one morning when he spilled some boiling water on his foot. He did not feel the slightest pain. At that moment he knew he was doomed. Leprosy destroyed his capacity to feel pain. Being able to feel pain was the clue that death had come to his body and little by little would take possession. How much better for him if that boiling water had caused him pain.

It is like the man whose feet had been amputated, who told of his experience being caught out in the bitter cold of the far north. So long as his feet pained him he was happy, but after a while, the pain was gone, and he knew then that his feet were doomed. The pain diminished as they froze.

How deadly, how horrible to be unable to feel the pain of our loss and the losses of others. And how pathetic not to be able to grieve the things we have done wrong to others. Socrates described a man's conscience as the wife from whom there is no divorce. Or there is the story of the little boy who, having been told by his father that conscience is a small voice which talks to us when we have done wrong, prayed, "Dear God, make the little voice loud." Experiencing our pain and that of those around us is the route to this blessing.

These words of Jesus are about loss that has happened to us personally. We are also to mourn what we have done which we should not have done, and we are to mourn the lost opportunities to help others that have passed us by. Blessed are they who mourn their sins.

During the Civil War, Abraham Lincoln proclaimed Thursday, April 30, 1863, as a national day of humiliation and prayer. Lincoln wrote: "It is the duty of nations as well as of men to own their dependence on the overruling power of God; to confess their sins and transgressions in humble sorrow … we have become too self-sufficient to feel the necessity and too proud to the God that made us."

This beatitude involves grieving personal loss, grieving our own behavior, and grieving the conditions of humanity. There is a sermon which I have never written that I am going to write some day titled "Too Sensitive to be Sane." No one should be more concerned about the pain and suffering of the world than we. This beatitude can be translated something like this: "Blessed are those who are particularly sensitive to the sin in themselves and in society, and who feel deeply all the distress caused by the ambition, greed, selfishness, hatred, and violence of the world."

This is a beatitude about our own pain and the pain of the world Jesus died to save. Blessed are they that share their neighbor's

19

pain and who mourn their pain as Jesus did, weeping over the sins of Jerusalem.

We all know people, and there are probably some here today, who mourn and are not comforted. We all know people whose grief seems not just to continue but to grow. What is missing? Have they gotten stuck in one of the first four stages of grief? Perhaps. We need to remember that this promise of comfort was made by Jesus. God is the source of comfort. The Messiah is the messenger of comfort. The promise of the Holy Spirit is the promise of the Holy Comforter. It is from God that this comfort is to be sought. As disciples of Christ, we are the vehicles God uses to bring the ministry of Christ and the comfort of the Holy Spirit. Comfort may not have been received because we have not sought the God who is the source of comfort, and because we have not opened ourselves to the channels by which God sends comfort.

According to a Buddhist legend, centuries ago a woman in grief over her dead child went to Buddha to plead that the child might be returned to life. Buddha sent her on a strange mission, promising to minister to her need when she returned. She was to go and collect a bowl of peppers from families who had not experienced grief such as hers. Mystified, but desperate for help, she undertook the unusual assignment. However, when evening came, the woman returned with an empty bowl, but herself filled with understanding.[1]

Mourning tends to be a very personal thing, but it does not have to be private. In our grief, when we isolate ourselves from others, we keep ourselves from the channels God uses to bring us comfort. Several years ago, in a tragic accident, my wife's brother Charlie was hit and killed by a school bus. The loss was an unspeakable tragedy for the family. You just never get over something like this.

It was just a few weeks later in the same town that another boy who was out delivering newspapers was struck by a car and he also died. Word spread quickly. As soon as Elise's father heard the news, he immediately went to that family's home. He was greeted at the door by a grief-stricken father. The man did not know who he was even though they went to the same church and lived in the same town. But when he introduced himself as the man whose son had been killed a short time before, the other father threw his arms around him. The two stood there for some time holding one another and crying together. They comforted one another.

Their comfort came out of sharing together their separate but similar tragedies. When Jesus taught these words he taught them to the gathered community. These are not private lessons. They are instructions to the community gathered in Jesus' name. When we mourn together in community, when we share our common grief, when we embrace one another, when we call on the presence and power of God, then in God's time God grants us comfort.

I believe mourning is not something we can do by ourselves. If all is well in our lives and world, we can go along thinking ourselves very much in control, but tragic loss forces us to seek strength and consolation beyond ourselves. Blessed is the person who cares intensely for the suffering and the sorrows and the needs of others. Blessed is the one who knows God is the ultimate source of our comfort. Mourning is a response of deep concern, of tender care. It is a godly sorrow. And God has promised that in sharing our sorrow, we shall be strengthened and encouraged.

When I was working as the chaplain of an adolescent psychiatric hospital, I was asked to lead a group for patients who were having a lot of trouble dealing with loss. These were youth ages ten to seventeen. I began by asking what kinds of losses they had had in their young lives. I was surprised to discover that every single one of them had experienced a significant loss through death and that they all still had serious unresolved issues about that loss. They did not know how to mourn, and so I was called in to help them do so. Many of them had been at that hospital for months, but secular treatment had not been able to adequately help them deal with their grief. Understanding and calling on the promise of God is necessary to receive the needed comfort.

A short time later at another adolescent treatment center on the other side of the city, a teenage patient committed suicide. This is an excellent hospital with highly trained psychiatrists, psychologists, social workers, nurses, and other treatment professionals. They did all they knew how to do to help these teenagers deal with their friend's death. But their staff realized that whatever they did was not enough, and so they called on me, not because I am a recognized expert, but because they knew there was something essential missing in their approach. I met with the teenagers for some time, discussing their loss not out of a psychological understanding, but out of a faith understanding because mourning that is given to God gets back in God's time God's promised comfort.

Like all the other beatitudes, this is a future-looking promise. A Catholic priest by the name of Henri Nouwen wrote a little book titled *A Letter of Consolation*. It was written from a son to a father six months after the death of the son's — Henry — mother. At one point he said, "The Lord who died, died for us … for you, for me, for mother, and for all people. He died not because of any death or darkness in him, but only to free us from the death and darkness in us. If the God who revealed life to us, and whose only desire is to bring us life, loved us so much that he wanted to experience with us the total absurdity of death, then, yes, there must be hope; then there must be something more than death; then there must be a promise that is not fulfilled in our short existence in this world; then leaving behind the ones you love, the flowers and the trees, the mountains and the oceans, the beauty of art and music, and all the exuberant gifts of life cannot be just the destruction and cruel end of all things; then indeed we have to wait for the third day."

The Greek word translated as "comfort" means "to call to the side of." This is mourning which calls us to the side of God to receive the comfort given by God. Mourning is a way to God's presence to receive God's blessing.

In giving our grief and mourning to God, we live with the confidence that what the gospel says is true. It is true what Paul wrote to the church, "If we live, we live to the Lord, and if we die, we die to the Lord; so then, whether we live or whether we die, we are the Lord's. For to this end Christ died and lived again, that he might be Lord both of the dead and of the living" (Romans 14:8-9). It is the ministry of this Lord "to comfort all who mourn" (Isaiah 61:2).

"How blest are the sorrowful; they shall find consolation." (NEB)

"Blessed is the one whose heart is broken for the world's suffering and for his own sin, for out of his sorrow he will find the joy of God!" (Barclay)

"Happy are those who have a god-like sympathy toward their fellow man. They shall have the assurance that God cares for them." (Guth, *The Pulpit* 12/54)

"Happy are they who bear their share of the world's pain: in the long run, they will know more happiness than those who avoid it." (*The Pulpit* 12/59)

"Blessed are those who mourn, for if they could not mourn, they could not love. Blessed are those who do not try to escape pain and suffering, but face it, seeking for its message, letting it bring forth the humanness within them." (*The Pulpit* 10/66)

"Blessed are those who mourn, for they shall be comforted." (RSV)

---

1. Edgar N. Jackson, *You And Your Grief* (Manhasset, N.Y.: Channel, 1961), pp. 61-62.

3

The Meek

Psalm 37:1-11
Matthew 5:1-12

This is not the beatitude of anyone claiming "I am the greatest." In fact, like all the other beatitudes, we have to wonder how practical these words are. What business could survive being meek? This is not a slogan you are likely to find above the door to the Stock Exchange on Wall Street. Meekness will not win the play-off series between the New York Knicks and the Chicago Bulls. We tend to think of the meek as the casualties, not as the winners. "Miserable are the meek, because they get trampled upon." We live in a world of assertiveness training. We live in a world which values getting what you want and then wanting more. There are countless courses, books, and television shows about getting what is "due" to you. And a good part of the growth in our national debt is from folks insisting on getting what they consider to be their entitlements.

In the television series *M*A*S*H 4077*, Father Mulcahy was taking out his frustration on everyone when once again he was passed over for a promotion. Colonel Potter was almost as upset as Father Mulcahy. Potter called the Pentagon to complain and insist that Mulcahy get his promotion. The Colonel got his way and the promotion was granted. As the award was pinned on him, Mulcahy said, "This has taught me that the meek may inherit the earth, but it is the grumpy who get promoted."

"Happy are they who complain, for they get their own way in the end." There is a story which made the rounds several years ago which goes like this. It seems that the postmaster in Washington, D.C., forwarded a letter that was addressed to Lord God Almighty to Monsignor Sheen. It asked the Lord God

25

Almighty to send $50 immediately. "I sent the man who wrote it $25," reported Monsignor Sheen, "so he wouldn't lose his faith in God."

A couple of weeks later the postmaster forwarded another letter to Monsignor Sheen, addressed in the same way and from the same man. It again asked for $50. This time the man wrote, "Next time, Lord, you better send the money through Cardinal Spellman, because last time Monsignor Sheen held back $25 on me." "Happy are they who complain, for they get their own way in the end."

The word we render as "meek" is difficult to translate from the original Greek into English. We tend to link the works "meek" and "little," as in "he is a meek, little man." There are unfortunate implications with the word "meek" which imply a meek person is without courage, or self-respect, a broken-spirited person.

The Reverend David H.C. Read (in *The Pattern of Christ*) tells us of being informed while he was at a Scottish church that a certain young man was going to enter the ministry. The person relaying this information said to him, "I am so pleased. He's just the type (to be a pastor) — a nice, harmless boy."

At the time the Greek word "praeis" was first translated into English, the word "meek" had a different meaning than it does today. Once upon a time the word "meek" characterized a person who was free of self-will, someone who wasn't interested in getting his or her own way, but was interested in the good of other people.

This is a word that only makes sense today when it is understood as describing the relationship between God and ourselves, not simply a description of how people relate to one another. The Greek word which we translate as "meek" was used to describe a horse that was bridled, ready to run a race. The meek are those disciplined and controlled by God, ready to run God's race.

To be meek people is to believe that God is in charge of our lives and to let God control and direct our lives just as a horse lets its owner take charge of the bridle. When God is in control, then the whole earth is ours. Meekness is not weakness. It is a word that denotes self-control. It is a gentle, controlled, disciplined spirit.

To be meek does not mean we are without feeling. Aristotle spoke of meekness as the place between anger and indifference.

The meek are permitted to be angry. It is not a selfish anger in which we become angry at wrong done to us. It is a selfless anger at the wrong done to others. It comes from a control that is beyond our control. It is a God-controlled life. While others are fighting to get what they believe is due them, the meek are more concerned about their duties. As opposed to those who assert the pride of race, the pride of power, the pride of knowledge, as opposed to those who demand their place in the sun, the meek are content to walk in the shadows where God keeps watch over them. What they ultimately receive is far greater. Not being puffed up with their own self-importance, they become teachable. Quintilian was a great Roman teacher of oratory who said of certain scholars, "They would no doubt be excellent students if they were not already convinced of their own knowledge." "Blessed is the person who has the humility to know his own ignorance, his own weakness, and his own need."

To be meek is to be controlled. Meekness brings with it the ability to control our feelings and inclinations so we are bridled and can act according to God's will and way. To be meek, to give ourselves over to God's will, we receive what others only long for. It was Dante who said, "In His will is our peace."

It reminds me of some advice I received at a seminar I once attended. The seminar was designed for the staff at a psychiatric hospital to help them relate better to patients. The issue came up of what to do if you found yourself in a tug-of-war with a patient over some issue. Various people came up with ideas on how to win the tug-of-war. Some advice sounded pretty good. Other ideas sounded rather extreme. The leader's advice was simple. He said, "If you find yourself in a tug-of-war with someone, the easiest way to end the tug-of-war is to let go of the rope."

Meek people are those who, in surrendering to God, avoid foolish power struggles and are given back great strength. Moses, who stood alone before all the power of Pharaoh and led an entire people to freedom, was described as being meek (Numbers 12:3). To his contemporaries, Jesus was never accused of being a wimp. He was viewed as a troublemaker, and that is why he was crucified. Yet, he referred to himself as meek. "Take my yoke upon you and learn of me. For I am meek" (Matthew 11:29 KJV).

27

Consider these descriptions of the meek:

"People ... who instinctively react with love are the meek. The person who is too weak to love when it hurts thinks that meek people are afraid. They are, in a way, but they are afraid of hating. It is easier to hate, sometimes, than to love, and meek people have to be strong. People who are not meek stop loving when it hurts." Russell Criddle, *Love Is Not Blind*

"The meek are not those who never get angry, for such are insensible, but those who, feeling anger, control it, and are angry only when they ought to be. Meekness excludes revenge, irritability, morbid sensitiveness, but not self-defense, or a quiet and steady maintenance of right." Theophylact

"God has two dwellings; one in heaven, and the other in a meek and thankful heart." Izaak Walton

"Selfish men may possess the earth; it is the meek only who inherit it from the Heavenly Father, free from all defilements and perplexities of unrighteousness." Woolman

"Meekness is love at school, at the school of Christ. It is the disciple learning to know, and fear, and distrust himself, and learning of him who is meek and lowly in heart, and so finding rest in his soul." J. Hamilton

"Meekness cannot well be counterfeited. It is not insensitivity, or unmanliness, or whine. It is benevolence imitating Christ in patience, forbearance, and quietness. It feels keenly, but not malignantly; it abounds in good will, and bears all things." W.S. Plumber

We can become over-familiar with the words of the beatitudes — the meek shall inherit the earth — and not notice how startling this reward is. The meek get it all. They will inherit the whole earth. They are not going to earn it or win it or conquer it. They will simply inherit the world. It is a gift, the reward for meekness.

If this is true, then it is a matter of serious concern for us. If you knew you were going to inherit an enormous estate if you had only one particular character trait, you would be very concerned about that. Like the other beatitudes, the key to understanding this is to put it in God's time, and know it will be achieved in God's way. This is not a blessing to be received by a David Koresh through armed conflict with federal authorities. This is a difficult blessing because our inclination is to dominate and control other people. Meekness is so rare a quality because so many want to win the earth for themselves.

The disciples who first heard these words were citizens of a nation which was being held captive by Roman soldiers. They were being heavily taxed by a foreign oppressor. We know how infuriated people become when elected officials seek to raise taxes. We can only imagine how furious people would be toward taxes raised by a foreign dictator for the benefit of the oppressor. Just how welcome would the blessing of meekness be to the people of that land? In fact, this blessing must have seemed to many listening as infuriating and untrue. Yet, time has proven this truth.

There is a one-act play written by Charles R. Kenney titled *The Terrible Meek*. It takes place at Calvary. There are three characters: a soldier, his captain, and Mary, the mother of Jesus. The captain and the soldier nailed Jesus to the cross, watched him dying in agony, then finished him with a thrust of the spear into his heart. After the crowd departed and night came over the hill, the captain and the soldier became uneasy over what they had done. They wondered why they had just done this terrible deed and could find no reason for it except they had been ordered to do so.

The presence and power of Jesus began to shatter their cold obligation to duty. After a great struggle of the soul, the captain finally turned to Jesus' mother and said, "We stretch out our hands to possess the earth — domination, power, glory, money, merchandise, luxury — these are the things we aim at; but what we really gain is pestilence and famine, crude labor, the enslaved hate of men and women, ghosts, dead and death-breeding ghosts that haunt our lives forever. We have lost both the earth and ourselves in trying to possess it."

29

Then he concluded, "I tell you, woman, this dead son of yours, disfigured, shamed, spat upon, has built a kingdom this day that can never die. The living glory of him rules it. The earth is his and he made it. He and his brothers have been molding and making it through the long ages; they are the only ones who ever really can possess it: not the proud, not the idle, not the wealthy, not the vaunting empires of the world. Something has happened up here on this hill today to shake all our kingdoms of blood and fear to dust ... the meek, the terrible meek, the fierce, agonizing meek, are about to enter into their inheritance."[1]

"How blessed are those of gentle spirit...." (NEB)

"Happy are those who realize that they do not know everything and are willing to learn from God. They shall be the great leaders." (*The Pulpit* 12/54)

"Happy are those who accept life and their own limitations: they will find more in life than anybody." (*The Pulpit* 12/29)

"Congratulations to the meek; they are receiving even at present God's inheritance, the gift of life to the fullest. They are discovering life in the full dimension which God has built into it."

"Happy is the man who submits his life in obedience to the will of God, for God will lead him into the fullness of life he intends for his children."

"Blessed are they who obey God, for they shall inherit the earth." (Van Blair)

"Blessed are the humble-minded for they will possess the land." (Goodspeed)

"O the bliss of the person who is always angry at the right time and never angry at the wrong time, who has every instinct, every impulse, every passion under control because he himself is God-controlled, who has the humility to realize his own ignorance and his own weakness, for such a man is a king among others." (Barclay)

"Blessed are the meek, for they shall inherit the earth." (RSV)

---

1. Charles R. Kenney, *The Terrible Meek* (New York: Samuel French, Inc., 1933). *The Terrible Meek* by Charles Raan Kenney, copyright 1912, 1933, 1939 by Charles Raan Kenney, copyright 1961 (renewal) by Harold J. Gorst. All rights strictly reserved. Used by permission.

4

The Righteous

Psalm 107:36-41
Matthew 5:1-12

I have never been to the Holy Land, but I have heard the land described. The "desert" in Palestine is not made up of sand dunes, but of parched, rock-filled crusty soil. It quickly turns to dust in the long dry seasons. This is an arid land where water was used only for the most essential needs. When the rain falls, the thirsty land is satisfied and in a few days the land rejoices with blossoms shooting up everywhere in beautiful array. Soon again the dry season returns, the harvest ends, and the problems of hunger and thirst return to the people.

Satisfying thirst is, quite literally, a matter of life and death. Jesus fed human hungers. He fed the hunger with food: He taught us to pray for our daily bread. It is hard for us to understand the hunger and thirst those people felt and many today still feel. Most of us suffer from what Robert Louis Stevenson referred to as "the malady of not wanting." Few of us really know what it is like to live with a life-threatening scarcity of food and water.

Like the other beatitudes, this may have seemed like a nonsense statement to the first listeners. Life was lived on the edge of starvation. Bread and water were precious commodities. People would hardly find their hunger and thirst satisfied with something as abstract as "righteousness."

In one manner or another, we all have hungers and thirsts we seek to satisfy. But we can seek satisfaction in ways that never remain satisfying. I once spoke with a man who owned a chemical company. He told me about chemicals he sold to beverage makers that they put in their drinks so that our thirst is never quite quenched. Remember the ad that had as its slogan, "The one beer to have

33

when you're having more than one"? Is it surprising that bars serve salty pretzels and peanuts to increase thirst rather than satisfy it?

We are too easily content with a satisfying moment, but do not strive for a satisfying life. When we have a cheeseburger and a Coke, we feel filled for a while, but want something else soon after. Within an hour or two of the close of this service, most of us begin craving food and drink. We do that every day, usually many times a day. Here Jesus challenges us not just to make things right with our need for nourishment, but to make things right for a hungry world, to crave a world that is right and just, as often and as intently as we crave food and drink.

This is a challenge to examine that for which we hunger and thirst. John Stuart Mill said his life was changed by his suddenly asking himself this question: "Suppose I attain what I am now pursuing. What sort of man shall I be at the end?"

Jesus promised that there is a way of satisfying the hunger of the soul just as we crave to satisfy the hunger of the body. We try to satisfy ourselves with what we can see and smell and taste, but Saint Paul said, "No eye has seen, nor ear heard, nor the heart of man conceived what God has prepared for those who love him" (1 Corinthians 2:9).

Hunger continues to be a terrible tragedy. Consider this image. A DC-10 is preparing to land. It is filled with small children. Some of the children sleep; others play and laugh; still others cry out for the harried flight attendant's attention. But just before landing something goes wrong and the plane plummets to the ground, killing all aboard.

Ten minutes later — even before the emergency vehicles arrive — another planeload of children crashes right next to the first. Ten minutes later, a third crashes. And the tragedies continue: every ten minutes, a jet falls to earth, all day and night, day after day, month after month. Such a great number of deaths is not far-fetched. The same number of children — 40,000 — die each day from hunger-related diseases.[1]

Jesus wants these human hungers to be satisfied, for things to be put right with the world, so that no child ever goes to bed hungry at night. At one point, Jesus criticized people for saying "Peace, peace" when there is no peace. Feeling content because we are well fed can keep us from feeling the unquenchable hunger and thirst of a needy world. We cannot be content with anything less than the peace and righteousness of God's kingdom. Blessed are the dissatisfied. Blessed are those who possess a divine discontent. Blessed are those who restlessly hunger and thirst for a more just and peaceful world. Blessed are those who refuse to be satisfied with things the way they are and call us to do the right thing.

There is a story of a young man who came to Buddha seeking the true way of life, the path of righteousness. Buddha led him down to the river. The young man assumed that he was to undergo some ritual of purification, some type of baptismal service.

They walked out into the river for some distance and suddenly Buddha grabbed the man and held his head under the water. Finally, in a last gasp, the fellow wrenched himself loose and his head came above the water. Quietly Buddha asked him, "When you thought you were drowning, what did you desire most?" The young man gasped, "Air." Buddha replied, "When you want righteousness as much as you wanted air, then you will get it."[2]

Blessed are those who hunger and thirst for righteousness, for they shall be satisfied. Jesus did not say, "Blessed are the righteous. They have all the virtue they need." That is like telling students they have learned all they need to know. They will stop studying.

Jesus was concerned that we are personally righteous. Our behavior and attitudes are important. Righteous living is important just as righteous living is dangerous. Once the great British preacher Charles Spurgeon received a letter from a man who declared that if he did not receive a certain sum of money from the preacher within two days, he would publish certain things that would end Spurgeon's influence. Spurgeon wrote back, "You, and your like, are requested to publish all you know about me across the heavens." How satisfying to have a personal rightness with God that everything about one could become public knowledge and cause no scandal.

When Jesus spoke, righteousness was commonly measured by what took place in the temple and the synagogue. It was measured by your attendance and contributions, and by keeping countless rules, traditions, and laws that had been added over the years by various religious leaders. For us to simply reduce this to "righteous" behavior avoids its larger meaning, and eliminates our hungering and thirsting for it, since we can convince ourselves we already have it.

That kind of righteousness is like perfume that makes you smell sweet, but really isn't part of you. This practice of religion was compared by Clarence Jordon to wearing a necktie and coat to church on a hot summer day. It is uncomfortable, but may seem necessary to appear respectable. These are social customs that fill certain social expectations, but do not fill our spirits.

It is like the rather pious churchman who was criticizing his neighbor for the neighbor's profanity. The profane neighbor replied, "Well, my friend, I cuss a lot and you pray a lot, but neither of us really means what he says."

Or it is like the story of a convicted criminal, a rough-looking character his fellow prison inmates nicknamed Spike. Just before his release from prison after serving a fifteen-year sentence, Spike had a long talk with the prison chaplain. He told the chaplain how much he looked forward for all those years to the time when he could hold up his head in society and live a good life.

Among other things, the chaplain advised Spike to join the church nearest to his home as soon as he was released. It so happened that the church nearest to the ex-convict's apartment was located on the edge of the rich area.

Spike called on the pastor of this fashionable church and told him of his desire to join. "My dear man," said the pastor, with more than a touch of superiority, "I do not think you would be happy here, though I appreciate your good intentions. Really, you would be most uncomfortable amongst my people and I am afraid it would be quite embarrassing to you and perhaps to them. I suggest you think it over and pray and meditate and see if God does not give you some direction."

A week later, Spike met the pastor on the street, stopped him, and said, "Reverend, I took your advice and prayed and meditated and finally God sent me word. He said I should not bother any more trying to join your church. God said He Himself has been trying to get in there for years without success."

Jesus was not primarily referring to a striving for personal holiness which tends toward illusions of self-righteousness. The word "righteousness" sometimes refers to us having a right relationship with God and a right relationship with God's people.

We are to long for the world to be right, for there to be a victory of good over evil. It is not looking so much for peace within as for peace to be spread abroad in the world. We cannot be content with how righteous we are, because the righteousness of which Jesus spoke is measured by doing right for others.

The blessed hunger and thirst are not to satisfy our own hunger and thirst. When we hunger for a ham sandwich and a cup of coffee, we also need to feel hunger and thirst for the hungry to be fed and the homeless to be housed. The blessing of this satisfaction is only achieved by dissatisfaction, hungering to do what is right for God and the world, not just for ourselves. To satisfy our own hunger has its own reward. To hunger and thirst for the world to be right is the source of the blessing.

To hunger and to thirst indicates an intense desire. It is like the expression, "I want it so bad I can taste it." But it does not mean we have achieved what we have set out to do. This is not saying, "Blessed are the righteous," but "blessed are those who hunger and thirst for righteousness." It is like God saying to David "Whereas it was in your heart to build a house for my name, you did well that it was in your heart" (1 Kings 8:18). It is like Robert Louis Stevenson's comment that "to travel hopefully is a better thing than to arrive."

It is like children at play who want more than anything to be Michael Jordan slam-dunking a basketball. They will never be the player he is, but in hungering and thirsting to be like him, they continue to strive to play better and better.

It was in 1985 that singer/songwriter Bob Geldof organized the Live Aid benefit concert to feed the hungry. Geldof, lead singer of a rock group with the marvelous name of "Boomtown Rats," recruited the cream of British pop talent to record a song he co-wrote called "Do They Know It's Christmas?" Then he helped organize the dual continent Live Aid extravaganza which raised several million dollars. The theme song of that was "We Are the World." When receiving a reward for this, Geldof's comment was, "What these efforts have done is to make compassion hip again."

Predictably, this compassion for the hungry is, to continue the food metaphor, on the back burner. Feeding the hungry was high fashion for a brief season. Now it is on to other politically correct causes. This blessing does not come to those who are content that they have done enough, who then move on to another cause, any more than we can believe that today's lunch is all the food we will ever need. It is the divine discontent with an unrighteous world which leads us forever toward the promise of this blessing.

"Happy are those who want God's approval as desperately as a dying man, stumbling toward a desert mirage, wants a drink, or as a starving man longs for a crust of bread. They shall receive that which they seek." (*The Pulpit* 12/54)

"Blessed are they which do hunger and thirst after righteousness, for they shall be filled." (KJV)

"O the bliss of the man who longs for total righteousness as a starving man longs for food, and a man perishing of thirst longs for water, for that man will be truly satisfied." (Barclay)

"Blessed are they who hunger and thirst for it, for they shall find that it meets their deepest needs." (Jordon)

"Blessed are those who hunger and thirst for righteousness, for they shall be satisfied." (RSV)

---

1. Tom Peterson, "Child Survival," *The Christian Century,* 7/1/87.

2. Told by Dr. Ralph Sockman, recorded in Allen, *God's Psychiatry.*

5

The Merciful

Matthew 5:1-12
Matthew 18:23-35

The quality of mercy is not strain'd,
It droppeth as a gentle rain from heaven
Upon the place beneath: it is twice blest;
It blesseth him that gives and him that takes:
'Tis mightiest in the mightiest: it becomes
The throned monarch better than his crown.
(The Merchant of Venice, Act IV, scene 1)

In our practice of "mercy" there is a kind of "I'll scratch your back — you scratch my back" philosophy. Be decent to others and they will be decent to you. It is like the story on which George Bernard Shaw based his play *Androcles and the Lion.* Androcles was a Roman slave who lived in the days of the Emperor Tiberius. He ran away from a cruel master and took refuge in a cave. A lion came wandering by, limping badly. He held out the damaged paw to Androcles, who skillfully extracted a huge thorn.

Scene two took place some time later. Poor Androcles had been caught and was being thrown to the wild beasts in the circus. But the lion sent to devour him turned out to be his old friend. So, instead of attacking him, the lion nuzzled up and began to caress him, whereupon the crowd was so astonished that Androcles was set free. Happy ending. And a tale of fantasy.

Christians are not to be merciful because there is some payback system. If I lend my neighbor my hedge clippers when his break, then I can borrow his lawn mower when mine stops working. We are not merciful to receive reward but we are merciful simply because God is merciful. We are merciful because we are committed to act like Jesus and he was filled with mercy. The mercy of which Jesus speaks is the attitude of someone who not only acts expecting nothing back, but who knows he may receive abuse for his act of mercy.

Acts of mercy are not always rewarded with gratitude. In this world the merciful are often devoured by the lions, even those whom they have helped. We live in a world where the merciful get taken for suckers, where kindness can be seen as character weakness. No one showed more mercy than Jesus. Jesus' reward for showing mercy was the betrayal of his closest friends, condemnation by religious and political leaders, flogging by soldiers, and death on a cross.

As Balzac said, "Society, like the Roman youth at the circus, never shows mercy to the fallen gladiator." Which reminds me of the story of a mother who was appalled and angry that her daughter had gotten into a fight at school. The mother said, "That is not how I taught you to behave. The devil must have made you do it!" Her daughter replied, "Maybe so, but kicking her in the shins was MY idea."

Refusing to show mercy is compared with breaking down the bridge over which you yourself would have passed. In God's system of justice, we receive the mercy or judgment we give others. Several years ago, Lavrenti Beria, the former chief of the Russian Secret Police, was arrested and "liquidated." He became the victim of his own actions. Locked in the prison where he had locked others, subjected to treatment that he had taught his secret police, tried in the sort of trial he had helped to engineer, he was mocked by his own cruelty.

We know the blessing of this beatitude, but we need also to consider the warning of the parable. In March of 1976, Carlo Gambino, boss of all bosses of the Mafia, died in New York. He was the model for the role of Don Vito Corleone, the part played by Marlon Brando in the movie *The Godfather.* We lived in New York City at the time of Gambino's death. In a local news report, it said that the funeral service included the words "Be not severe in Thy judgment."

Think of the souls and bodies scarred and killed by what he did — the youth seduced into drugs, countless people led into crime,

42

the women forced into prostitution, the politicians corrupted, the businesses compromised and destroyed. We can ask for God's mercy, but that does not cancel out God's judgment. Our God is a God of mercy, but when we expect to receive mercy without giving mercy, the parable tells us about the nature of God's judgment. When we live a life without mercy, we live a life without hope. There is a communion prayer whose words include these: "We are not worthy so much as to gather up the crumbs under Thy table. But Thou art the same Lord whose property is always to have mercy." Mercy is what God seeks to give, but when we are unmerciful, we block God's mercy.

It is what we pray for each time we pray the Lord's Prayer: "Forgive us our debts as we forgive our debtors." After teaching us to pray for forgiveness, Jesus added: "For if you forgive men their trespasses, your heavenly Father also will forgive you; but if you do not forgive men their trespasses, neither will your Father forgive your trespasses."

This beatitude marks a shift from the passive to the active, from the poor in spirit, those who mourn, the meek, those hungry and thirsting, to acts of mercy. Mercy is active. It is not a passive "Oh, gee, isn't that too bad." Mercy is active. It is reaching out to the suffering of the world. It is carrying the basket of food to the hungry family. It is dialing the telephone to check on a lonely neighbor. It is stopping at the roadside to change the tire of a woman traveling with her little children.

This is the beatitude of the givers, of the charitable. This refers to those who have such an attitude of compassion toward others that they want to share gladly all that they have. It does not view the needy as beggars to whom we give just a little bit, but brothers and sisters with whom we share all. This understanding of charity or mercy led some of the early Christians to a state of voluntary poverty in which "all the believers were together and held all things in common" (Acts 2:44).

Mercy is not simply feeling sorry for someone. "I am sorry your cat is sick." It is more than an emotional wave of pity. It is a profound sympathy, being with others in their pain. There is a story about Queen Victoria of England. She was a close friend of

43

Principal and Mrs. Tulloch of St. Andrews. Prince Albert died and Queen Victoria was left alone. Just about the same time, Principal Tulloch died and Mrs. Tulloch was left alone.

Unannounced, Queen Victoria came to call on Mrs. Tulloch when Mrs. Tulloch was resting on a couch in her room. When the Queen was announced, Mrs. Tulloch struggled to rise quickly from the couch and to curtsy. The Queen stepped forward: "My dear," she said, "don't rise. I am not coming to you today as a queen to a subject, but as one woman who has lost her husband to another." That is what God did in the person of Jesus. He came not as a removed monarch, but as one of us. In his mercy, Jesus shared in our own pain.

And so this attitude of mercy is a mark of our nature as a Christian people. One of the leaders of the early church is named Tertullian. He had these words of insight and encouragement to the early church members: "It is our care for the helpless, our practice of loving-kindness that brand us in the eyes of many of our opponents. 'Look!' they say, 'How they love one another! Look how they are prepared to die for one another.' "

Mercy is shown to friends as well as to enemies. The merciful are those who banish all feelings of revenge and ill will out of their hearts, seeking to cultivate an attitude of love and sympathy toward all.

When Mother Teresa first began her work among the dying on the streets of Calcutta, India, she was obstructed at every turn by government officials and orthodox Hindus who were suspicious of her motives and used their authority to harass her and to frustrate her efforts. She and her fellow sisters were insulted and threatened with physical violence.

One day a shower of stones and bricks rained down on the women as they tried to bring the dying to their humble shelter. Eventually Mother Teresa dropped to her knees before the mob. "Kill me!" she cried in Bengali, her arms outstretched in a gesture of crucifixion. "And I'll be in heaven all the sooner." The crowd withdrew, but soon the harassment increased. Even more irrational acts of violence and louder demands were made of officials to expel the foreign nun in her white sari, wearing a cross around her neck.

One morning, Mother Teresa noticed a gathering of people outside the nearby Kali Temple, one of the holy places for Hindus in Calcutta. As she drew closer, she saw a man stretched out on the street with turned-up eyes and a face drained of blood. A triple braid denoted that he was of the Brahmin caste, not of the temple priests. No one dared to touch him, for people recognized he was dying from cholera. Mother Teresa went to him, bent down, took the body of the Brahmin priest in her arms and carried him to her shelter. Day and night, she nursed him; over and again he would say to the people, "For thirty years I have worshipped a Kali (god) of stone. But I have met in this gentle woman a real Kali, a Kali of flesh and blood." Never again were stones thrown at Mother Teresa and the other sisters.[1]

Mercy is a costly gift to give, not easily given, and often not a gift properly received. There is the story of the old mountaineer who was on trial for stealing a horse. He hired a good lawyer and the lawyer won the case. "You have been acquitted," said the lawyer. The mountaineer scratched his head and asked, "Does this mean I get to keep the horse?"

Or there is the spirit of the little boy who was protesting having to take a bath. His mother said, "You have dirt all over you. Don't you want to be clean?" The little boy inquired, "Can't you just dust me?" Mercy is a gift that can be taken most seriously or very lightly. Mercy is a great gift not because it takes sin lightly, but because it takes it so seriously.

A pastor told me how a member of the congregation he was serving had gone out one Friday night, gotten drunk, chased a young lady down an alley, and was then beaten up by the people who stopped him. Saturday morning this man's picture appeared on the front page of the local paper. The man's face was all banged up, his eyes were all puffy, and the picture was accompanied by a complete account of the incident.

When the pastor got a copy of the paper, he sat down, wrote this man a note, and sent his wife out to deliver it. The note read, "We would be most disappointed if we did not see you and your family sitting up front in church tomorrow." The next morning, they were there, facing all of the painful humiliation, paying all the emotional cost of being there. The pastor could have ignored him and the congregation shunned him. They could have stayed home alone with the shame and guilt. Instead, they were welcomed back and the one who was lost became found. Mercy was needed and mercy was shown. The quality of mercy is such that while considering a person dead wrong in what one has done, we can still offer compassion and forgiveness.

This is the nature of a merciful God. The mercy to which Jesus referred is not simply our being merciful to one another, but God being merciful to us. All acts of mercy have their origin with God. God is the source, the author, the creator of mercy.

There is a dual sense in which we receive mercy. We receive mercy now and in the kingdom. We know the joys of performing acts of mercy. We know the pleasure of receiving the merciful actions of others. In this world we will not always find mercy returned when mercy is shown. But in being merciful, we are sure, in God's time, to obtain mercy from God.

"The merciful are partakers of the divine blessing for they shall receive mercy." (Jordon)

"Happy are those who are always alert to the needs of others and do what they can to meet those needs. They shall find that God will take care of their needs." (*The Pulpit* 12/54)

"Happy are those who are ready to make allowances and to forgive: they will know the love of God." (*The Pulpit* 12/59)

"O the bliss of the man who gets right inside other people, until he can see with their eyes, think their thoughts, feel with their feelings, for he who does that will find others do the same for him, and will know that that is what God in Jesus Christ has done." (Barclay)

"The happy man is he who overlooks little slights and forgives large offenses."

"Blessed are the merciful, for they shall obtain mercy." (RSV)

---

1. Donald J. Shelby, "Weakness and Power," *Homiletics* 1/93 (Santa Monica, Calif.), p. 21c.

6

The Pure In Heart

Psalm 42
Matthew 5:1-12

Purity of heart is a common thead throughout scripture. The first of the Ten Commandments says: "You shall have no other gods before me" (Deuteronomy 5:7). In the Sermon on the Mount, Jesus said, "No one can serve two masters; for either he will hate the one and love the other, or he will be devoted to the one and despise the other" (Matthew 6:24). "Enter by the narrow gate; for the gate is wide and the way is easy, that leads to destruction, and those who enter by it are many. For the gate is narrow and the way is hard that leads to life, and those who find it are few" (Matthew 7:13-14).

And later he said, "The Kingdom of Heaven is like a merchant in search of fine pearls, who, on finding one pearl of great value, went and sold all that he had and bought it" (Matthew 13:45-46). And again, he said, "No one who puts his hand to the plow and looks back is fit for the Kingdom of God" (Luke 9:62).

Blessed are the pure in heart. We may think of the heart as the seat of emotion, but biblically, it refers to the center of our inner life, the mind as well as the emotions, the source of our will and decision making. To be pure is to be unmixed, without alloy. In Psalm 24:4, the pure in heart "does not lift up his soul to what is false, and does not swear deceitfully." It is to be a person of integrity, of unmixed motives, and singleness of purpose.

The nineteenth century Danish theologian Soren Kierkegaard summed it up in the title of his book *Purity of Heart Is to Will One Thing*. For the pure in heart, anything that gets in the way of that one thing must be put aside.

49

It is like a mother who went to her son's teacher to ask the teacher's help with a problem she was having. The mother said, "My son has horrible eating habits. Please speak with him. He will listen to you if you tell him to stop eating foods with so much sugar." The teacher listened sympathetically and said, "Please come back in a week and make the request again." The mother agreed and returned seven days later. "My son's problem continues," she said. "I am greatly concerned about his health. He rarely eats vegetables or fruits. Please, won't you talk to him about the danger of eating too much sugar?" The teacher again said, "Please come back and see me in a week."

Though the mother was disappointed, she left and returned one week later. Once again she made her plea. This time the teacher agreed to talk with her son. After the conversation was completed, the mother thanked the teacher. "I am grateful that you took the time to talk with my son, but I don't understand why it took three requests for you to do so." The teacher looked back at the mother and said, "I didn't realize how hard it would be for me to give up sugar." [1] The teacher could not teach the lesson with her lips without teaching the lesson with her life. Blessed are the pure in heart, for they shall help others see what God desires.

It is not uncommon for people to seek singleness of purpose. Perhaps at some time you have gone through goal setting for your life. Goals commonly include things like having adequate financial resources for retirement, career development, recreational or leisure goals.

In the early church they set goals that had to do with seeing God. The early church leader, Irenaeus (about 175 A.D.) said, "The glory of God is a living man; and the life of the man *is* the vision of God." [2] In the early church, the desire to have a vision of God became the goal of life and Christian conduct. Could there by any higher goal, any greater reason for purity of heart, than the desiring to see God wherever God is revealed?

When Phil Mitchell left here as pastor in 1972, he went on to write a wonderful little book entitled *Desire to See God*. [3] In the introduction he quoted Kahlil Gibran:

*And if you would know God be not therefore a solver of
riddles,
Rather look about you and you shall see Him playing
with your children.
And look into space; you shall see Him walking in the
cloud, outstretching His arms in the lightning and
descending in rain.
You shall see Him smiling in flowers, then rising and
waving.*

The title of the book — *Desire to See God* — is based on Phil's
personal longing to see God. Phil recalled the statement of the
disciple Philip, who at the last supper said, "Lord, show us the
Father and we shall be satisfied." Then Phil Mitchell told his own
story. As a seminary student there frequently came into his mind
doubts and confusion about his faith.

One evening he was sitting on the steps of the seminary library
looking up at the night sky. There was confusion in his mind and,
it seemed to him, confusion in the universe. He felt the agony of
wishing to believe in the reality of God, and a constant, persistent
desire for proof. He wanted just what his namesake, the disciple
Philip, wanted. He believed that if he could just see God, he would
be satisfied and life would be whole.

As he sat there, a friend came along whose name also happened
to be Philip. Phil Mitchell shared the heavy concerns of his heart
with the friend, saying, "I feel so immature, so childish in my faith.
All I seem to know of God is what I see of him in the lives of other
people. That's all that is convincing and it's so inadequate."

Of the statement this fellow student made in response, Phil
said, "No words have ever meant more to me than the words my
friend then uttered." The friend said, "Phil, no matter how God
chooses to reveal himself to you, never be ashamed of it." The
friend went into the library while Phil remained looking up at the
night sky. But this time, he did not see confusion in the stars.
Instead, he saw an orderly universe. And he wondered how he
had been so blind. God had always been present. The universe
had always had order. It was he who had failed to see God.

Phil concluded this section of his book with a paraphrase of Jesus' response to the request of the disciple Philip, who said, "Lord, show us the Father and we shall be satisfied." "O Philip, have you been so long a time with me and yet you do not know me! No one sees the Father, yet each act and word that expresses His will makes God known. Philip, can't you understand you have been seeing the Father all along as you lived with me? When you understand this, remember that when I leave you, people hungry for God will come to you with the same request, 'Show us the father.' Philip, do the works that I do and thus reveal God to others as I have revealed Him to you."

What a great blessing to be able to look and see the wonderful works of God. Last Friday, I went on the annual Hollis Elementary School third grade trip to the shore at Odiorn Point, N.H. We were there to go "tide pooling." Having grown up by the shores of Lake Erie, I did not know what I was in for. Other times I had walked along the rocky ocean shore. I had thought of tide pools as things to step over until I went with a group of trained and inquisitive third graders. Knowing what to look for, they could see and touch and hold all of the marvelous life that was there in God's created world.

It is easy to be blind to God's presence in the world, in our work and in the people around us. In the seventeenth century, there lived a man known as Brother Lawrence who wrote a series of letters compiled in a little book titled *The Practice of the Presence of God*. His letters tell of his struggle to see God even in the most menial of his kitchen tasks, tasks to which he had a great aversion. He practiced finding God present even in the midst of noisy confusion, opposition, and temptation.

And so he would repeat each day this simple prayer:

> *Lord of all pots and pans and things*
> *Since I've no time to be*
> *A saint by doing lovely things*
> *Or watching late with Thee,*
> *Or dreaming in the dawnlight,*
> *Or storming heaven's gate,*

Make me a saint by getting meals
And washing up my plate.

God can be seen in every situation, if we only have the eyes to see. There is a legend about the quest for the Holy Grail. The Holy Grail is the legendary cup used at the Last Supper, in which, it is reputed, that Joseph of Arimathea caught the last drop of blood which fell from Jesus' side as he died on the cross. Sir Galahad, along with other Knights of the Round Table, set out in quest of it. In the legend, they found it, but each saw it through the mirror of his own soul.

To some it was covered in mist and clouds. Their vision was very indistinct. Sir Lancelot saw it, but his heart was a sinful heart. He saw the Holy Grail covered with holy wrath and fire. To him, it was a vision of stern and awful retribution. Sir Galahad also saw the Holy Grail. He was the knight with the pure heart. It was said of him, "His strength was the strength of ten because his heart was pure." In the purity of his heart, he could see what to others was a horrible distortion. Blessed are the pure in heart, for they shall see God.

This is a wonderful promise, but it may also seem like the least accessible one of the beatitudes. We can be poor in spirit without wanting to be. We often mourn and feel meek. We can hunger and thirst for things to be right. We can act mercifully. But how do we go about being pure in heart? One pastor said that his reaction to this beatitude was not very positive. He said, "To tell me to be pure in heart seems about as helpful as for a doctor to say to me on discovering that my jugular vein was severed, 'My advice to you, young man, is that you stop bleeding.' " (Van Blare)

Jesus is talking about letting God take the heart and transform it. It is no easy thing for us to allow. It is so easy for us to substitute the practice of religion for the purity of heart. Purity of heart should not be confused with outward purity. Jesus was constantly troubled by those who put on a show of their goodness, but whose hearts were filled with evil thoughts and desires.

A characteristic of the pure in heart is sincerity. "Sincerity" comes from the Latin and literally means "without wax." In ancient

Rome devious dealers in marble and pottery would conceal defects in their products by filling the cracks and holes with wax. Honest merchants who did not do this displayed their wares as being "sina cera" — without wax. Some people put on a show to cover their personalities before they appear in public. The pure in heart do not cover up their flaws.

Moralists may think this beatitude is best described with the phrase, "Hear no evil, see no evil, speak no evil." There is a poem by Peter Olney which came from a time when the church had ruled dancing to be a sin. The poem goes like this:

> *Said the Reverend Joseph McCotten,*
> *"The Dance by the Devil's begotten."*
> *Said young John to Miss Shy,*
> *"Never mind that old guy —*
> *To the pure almost everything's rotten."*

Purity of heart is not a synonym for a spotless life or sterilized emotions. To be pure in heart is not the same as being morally perfect. None of us would qualify for that. I recently heard someone relate a comment from a pastor to an individual who was out searching for a church to join. The pastor said, "If you find a perfect church, don't join it. If you do, you'll ruin it." Or it is like the time Saint Peter halted a man at the entrance to heaven. Saint Peter said, "You've told too many lies to be permitted in here." "Have a heart," pleaded the man. "Remember, you were once a fisherman."

We are a forgiven people. Being pure in heart requires sincerity, admitting to God all our faults and giving God all of the garbage and baggage of past sins so we can get to what is really important. To be pure in heart is not to be heartless. It requires we have heart with all of the passions and emotions and longings. It is not simply using our will and forgetting our heart. Jesus was not trying to eliminate our emotion. Its purity comes with the discipline which keeps emotion from ruling our lives. The pure in heart have integrated the mind, emotion, and body to focus on a single goal. As the word "sin" literally means to miss the mark, the pure in

54

heart are those whose aim is true. To become pure in heart requires us to focus on seeing God in our life, letting nothing else stand in our way. This might be compared to a man running a race. He is determined that more than anything else, he will reach the tape across the finish line. As he runs, he hears some people booing him from the sidelines. He does not stop to argue or yell back. A little farther on somebody hits him as he goes by. He does not take the time or energy to stop and hit him back. Then, someone actually jumps out of the stands and tackles him. He rolls, breaks loose, gets up, and runs again. The tackler also gets up and runs after him, trying to tackle him again. But during the chase, the tackler discovers the joy of running and then, he too, sees the tape. Now two men run for the tape.

"Blessed is the person whose motives are always entirely unmixed, for that person shall see God." (Barclay)

"Happy are those who do only what God wants done. They shall have the greatest reward God can give—himself." (*The Pulpit* 12/ 54)

"Blessed are the pure in heart, for they shall see God." (RSV)

---

1. Reprinted from *Stories For The Journey* by William R. White, p. 96, copyright 1988 Augsburg Publishing House. Used by permission of Augsburg Fortress.

2. *Against Heresies,* IV, 34, 7.

3. Philip Mitchell, *Desire To See God* (Asbury Smith).

7

The Peacemakers

Ephesians 2:14-17
Matthew 5:1-12

"With malice toward none, with charity for all, with firmness in the right as God gives us to see the right, let us strive to finish the work we are in, to bind up the nation's wounds, to care for him who shall have borne the battle and for his widow and orphans, to do all which may achieve and cherish a just and a lasting peace among ourselves and with all nations." These are words from President Lincoln's second inaugural address, seeking to make peace after our nation's Civil War.

Being the bringer and maker of peace marked Jesus from the very beginning. At his birth the angels said, "Glory to God in the highest, and on earth peace, good will toward all." Instructions about peace are woven through this Sermon on the Mount: "Love your enemies and pray for those who persecute you" (Matthew 5:44). Peace was the bequest of Jesus in his last days. "Peace I leave with you, my peace I give you" (John 14:27). It is declared in the great music of the church that Jesus is the Prince of Peace. Central to the church's ministry of reconciliation is peacemaking.

We have inherited the Biblical vision of a peaceable kingdom. How close are we to achieving that? There is reportedly a zoo-keeper who, in the spirit of the peaceable kingdom described in the Old Testament by Isaiah, put in the same cage a lion and a lamb. Someone asked how he did it. He replied simply, "Every morning I put in a fresh lamb."

Peace is our vision, but war is more often our reality. Even the hope of peace may only seem possible through war. Those first hearing this beatitude were being held captive by Rome. They were not looking for peace. They were looking for a way to throw off the yoke of Roman oppression. They were yearning to be free of the foreign domination. They hoped for military leaders, not peacemakers. In the same way, many peoples and nations today refuse overtures of peace, seeing their only hope coming through the conflict of arms.

Yet even in war, the deepest longing is for peace. Saint Augustine said, "Peace is so great, that even in this earthly and mortal life there is no word we hear with such pleasure, nothing we desire with such zest, or find to be more thoroughly gratifying." Everyone is for peace just as everyone is for motherhood. But often when mothers lovingly do things they should do, their children do not respond in love. In the same way, when we do the things we should do that make for peace, it often leads to conflict.

We want peace. We want peace in our hearts. We want peace in our homes. We want peace in our church, in our neighborhood and in our world. We want a world where nation does not lift up sword against nation. We want homes where people are not battered emotionally or physically. We want to have peace. Agreeing on the need for peace is easy. The trouble comes when we do what Jesus said and try to *make* peace. The principle of peace is easy. Making peace is the hard part.

Over the years, there have been many who loved peace so much they ended up getting into fights over it. We have found those working for peace called "peacemongers." There is a terrible irony that within the church of the Prince of Peace the way to peace is often marked by dissension and discord. These are easier days for the church to talk about peace. Twenty-five years ago when the war in Vietnam was raging, to talk about peace in the church inevitably led to conflict. In other days when we find our soldiers in battle, it will again be difficult for those in the church to work for peace.

We often feel uncomfortable with the divisions peacemaking appears to cause. We are uncomfortable with charges of disloyalty to our nation as we try to speak on behalf of peace. The result is the cause of peace can suffer. We may become content with simply the absence of conflict. I may think that the world is at peace when my children do not have to sign up for the draft. Today they do not. But certainly the world is not at peace.

Being content with illusions of peace was condemned by the prophet Jeremiah when he said, "They have healed the wounds of my people lightly, saying, 'Peace, peace' when there is no peace" (Jeremiah 8:11). It is like the illusion of peace that occurred during the time of ancient Rome's power, the *Pax Romana,* a peace achieved only through ruthless military power and the suppression of all dissent. It is like Germany in the early 1930s when Hitler came to power. People said things like "I don't know anything about Hitler's politics, but I do know it is safe to go out in the streets again."

Dealing with peace in the political arena can be difficult. We can individually have little to do with achieving world peace. But we can work toward personal peace. We need to make peace with who and what we are. Within our souls we need to face the struggle between good and evil. There is a kind of civil war that rages within us. Saint Paul described it well when he said, "I do not understand my own actions. For I do not do what I want, but I do the very thing I hate. For I do not do the good I want, but the evil I do not want is what I do" (Romans 7:15, 19).

We need to be at peace with the situation which God has given us. We do need to experience the peace of God within ourselves to help us understand the peace of God within the world. There is a peace that is a kind of inner tranquillity. It is like the words of John Greenleaf Whittier's hymn:

> *Drop thy still dews of quietness,*
> *Till all our strivings cease;*
> *Take from our souls the strain and stress,*
> *And let our ordered lives confess*
> *The beauty of thy peace.*

This is not the peace of tranquilizers. This is not a peace that ends with settling inner conflict. I believe that one of the unfortunate limits of a lot of secular psychological therapy is that it ends when people feel good about themselves. Being a peacemaker only begins there. Being at peace with God and ourselves, Jesus then calls us to the blessing of being God's peacemakers in the world.

When you read through the literature written after the great wars in which our nation has fought this century, there is always the stated hope that this war will end wars, that this war will somehow be the battle that will finally bring us the peace for which we long. There is, I believe, little to be gained by looking back and second-guessing our national military actions. Evil is a powerful force, and there are times we have to protect people from the evil forces and evil people. Our leaders have done what they sincerely believed was the right thing to do. We have no capacity to judge what was in someone's heart when they acted as they did.

But there is a great benefit in looking ahead at the things we can do that make for peace. There is a godly blessing to be gained in modeling our lives after the life of the Prince of Peace. Jesus spoke of this very strange ethic which calls for loving our enemies and doing good to those who hate us. Instead of lifting up arms to fight our enemies, Jesus taught us to offer a hand to serve the enemy. When unjustly nailed on a cross, Jesus bore the cross and so for all time showed how to bear innocent suffering and showed how wrong it is to inflict suffering on any of God's people. That is his way of peace.

This is not a blessing achieved by going along with peace, or pointing out peace, or saying peace would be a good idea. This is not a blessing achieved by simply being peaceful or loving peace. This is the blessing of those who are out making peace. They are actively seeking to overcome evil with good.

Making peace requires action. Peace does not come from evading issues but from facing them. This is not the beatitude of those who passively accept things the way they are because they fear conflict. There is a difference between a peacemaker and a trouble-ducker. This beatitude does not say, "Blessed are those who are willing to live in the peace that someone else has established" (Pendleton). This is the beatitude of those who make peace because they are willing to face struggle.

We have inherited the biblical vision of a peaceable kingdom. How close are we to achieving that? It was the late General Omar Bradley who said, "Ours is a world of nuclear giants and ethical infants. We know more about war than we know about peace, more about killing than we know about living. We have grasped the mystery of the atom and rejected the Sermon on the Mount."[1]

Peacemaking is difficult work. Anything worthwhile is hard work. There is a story about George Lansbury, who was a tireless worker for peace in England. He had spent all of his adult life wrestling with the knotty problems which led England to war. He had lived through World War I and as he was dying, the guns of World War II were echoing through the world. To the realist it may have seemed as though he had thrown away his forty years of struggle. A close friend asked him how much nearer he thought peace was as a result of his effort. Lansbury answered, "Forty years nearer." [2]

Today, the United States is not officially committed to war, though there are several places our troops are active in combat or near combat situations. That does not mean we are at peace. Peace in the biblical understanding is much more than the absence of war. We can clear a piece of land of all its weeds, but that does not make it a garden. We can end armed conflict between adversaries, but ending armed conflict does not make them allies. Disarmament is a step toward peace, but not the final step. Destroying the sword and spear is the beginning, but it is making the swords into plowshares and the spears into pruning hooks that makes for peace.

It is for this blessing that we must hunger. When Ramsay MacDonald was Prime Minister of England, he was discussing with another government official the possibility of lasting peace. The official, an expert in foreign affairs, was unimpressed with Prime Minister MacDonald's idealistic viewpoint. He remarked cynically, "The desire for peace does not necessarily ensure it." This MacDonald admitted, saying, "Quite true. But neither does the desire for food satisfy your hunger, but at least it gets you started toward a restaurant." It is for this blessing that we must hunger.

"Blessed are the peacemakers, for they shall be called the children of God." This is the blessing, to be called the children of God. When I am asked to point out our sons, I often say, "They are the two who look nothing like me." Some of us bear a striking resemblance to our parents. Others look so different from their parents that you have to guess where they came from in the gene pool, or assume, as in our case, the children have been adopted. We are the children of God, made in God's image. It is not because God is a balding, white male who wears glasses. Being the children of God has nothing to do with outward appearance. It is not how we look but what we do that identifies our spiritual father. This blessing comes into being when people can look at what we are doing, seeing the peace we are making, and are able to see the nature of the God who created us.

Instead of being called children of God, peacemakers have often been called cowards while soldiers are called heroes. There is a cost to being a peacemaker. There are statues of military heroes. They are justly acknowledged. But where are the statues to the peacemakers? We honor and continue to honor those who served in battle, people of courage who fought for our freedom. A grateful nation thanks them. Successful military leaders are promoted and given titles.

For the peacemakers there is one reward and one title. God calls the peacemakers his own children. And that is their reward. Peacemakers seldom have statues and tributes and parades in their honor. The reward is being called God's child.

To be called a child of God means we bear God's very nature. The nature of God, as we know that through Jesus, is love, forgiveness and reconciliation. It is our God who is the creator of this peace. When the great Swiss theologian Karl Barth visited the United Nations, he said, "The international organization could be an earthly parable of the heavenly kingdom, but real peace will not be made here although it might seem as an approach. Peace will be made by God himself." To go out making peace we go out bearing the nature of God and living as members of God's kingdom. While war may seem to be the most terrible reality, for the children of God, the kingdom of God is the ultimate reality.

Leo Tolstoy told the story of a Russian youth, a conscientious objector to war, who stood trial. In the courthouse the young man expressed his position, declaring that his philosophy of life came from the demands of Christ. The judge replied, "Yes, I understand, but you must be realistic. These laws you are talking about are the laws of the Kingdom of God and it has not come yet!" The courageous young man answered, "Sir, I recognize that it has not come for you, nor yet for Russia, nor for the world. But it has come for me." And so we are called to living by an understanding and an ethical imperative that Jesus set apart in these beatitudes.

I was born during World War II. About that time a columnist in Chicago told of a London taxi driver by the name of Herbert Hodge who had come to Chicago for a visit. This man had suffered and seen all the horrors of the battles of London. As the newspaper columnist said, he had cause to want revenge. Yet when asked what he thought should be done to the Germans, he said simply, "Treat them like brothers, but take away their guns." [3] Our choices have been stated quite plainly that we can have peace or we can have revenge, but we cannot have both. For those who choose the way of making peace, Jesus offers this blessing.

"Happy are those who help others to live together; they will be known to be doing God's work." (*The Pulpit* 12/59)

"Happy are those who can express constructive good will toward one another. They are God's right-hand men." (*The Pulpit* 12/54)

"O the bliss of those who produce right relationships between man and man, for they are doing godlike work." (Barclay)

"Blessed are the peacemakers, for they shall be called children of God." (RSV)

---

1. Omar Bradley in *Quote* 9/1/81.

2. Bosley, *Preaching On Contemporary Issues*, p. 95.

3. *The Pulpit*, 11/43.

8

The Persecuted

Matthew 5:1-12
John 15:12-27

Jack Cahill, an advertising executive from Kansas City, Missouri, has suggested new marketing techniques which can help to tap the appeal to popular blessings. Beginning with the Roman Catholic Church (24 percent of the U.S. market), he suggests a strategy of market segmentation, a clear positioning of the church identifying specific subgroups within the brand name.

For the contemporary branch of the Roman Catholic Church, "the one that features hip priests, guitar playing, hand shaking, hugging, and other manifestations of universal niceness," he offers "R.C. Light"; for the conservative tradition, "R.C. Classic"; for the group most interested in liberation theology, "R.C. Free."

As for the Protestants, he says, "Many of the Protestant churches (PC's) have maintained a standback style since the Reformation and have been watching their market share shrink for about 400 years. After the big RC push, we can expect to see some of the more marginal, undifferentiated PC's go belly up."

To right the situation he suggests the individual churches will have to understand that there is just so much theological shelf space, that product differentiation is not viable for go-as-you-please Protestants. Currently, none of the mainstream Protestants — your Lutherans, your Episcopalians, your Southern Baptists, your Methodists — can really claim more than a ten percent market share.

He says, "My strategy is to consolidate the various brand names, even the strong flagship brands like Southern Baptist, into one identifiable Exxon-like entry. The target audience here is Mom, Dad, Butch, and Sis — solid suburban Americans who want a little God in their life and a place to go before brunch.

"And after test-marketing various possibilities, I have decided upon the name Middle American Christian Church, or 'MacChurch' for ad purposes. I will not be certain of MacChurch's theology until the focus groups are run, but I plan on following the promotional path blazed so successfully by Holiday Inn. In other words, this will be your basic 'no-surprise' church. When Dad brings the family here, he can be sure that they will not be asked to speak in tongues, handle snakes, or give money to the Sandinistas."

"Blessed are those who are *persecuted* for righteousness' sake." So said Jesus, but popular wisdom is quite different. Neil Postman, a Professor of Communication Arts and Sciences at New York University, wrote a book titled *Amusing Ourselves to Death: Public Discourse in the Age of Show Business*. In it, Professor Postman quotes the executive director of the National Religious Broadcasters Association, as he summed up what he calls the unwritten law of all television preachers: "You can get your share of the audience only by offering people what they want."

In response, Professor Postman wrote, "...This is an unusual religious credo. There is no great religious leader — from the Buddha to Moses to Jesus to Mohammed to Luther — who offered people what they wanted. Only what they needed. But television is not well suited to offering people what they need.

"It is user friendly. It is too easy to turn off. It is at its most alluring when it speaks the language of dynamic visual imagery. It does not accommodate complex language or stringent demands. As a consequence, what is preached on television is not anything like the Sermon on the Mount. Religious programs are filled with good cheer.

"They celebrate affluence. Their players become celebrities. Though their messages are trivial, the shows have high ratings, or rather *because* their messages are trivial, the shows have high ratings ... *Christianity is a demanding and serious religion. When it is delivered as easy and amusing, it is another kind of religion altogether.*"[1]

"Blessed are you when men revile you and persecute you and utter all kinds of evil against you falsely on my account." We are often willing to do so until it becomes inconvenient. Charles Allen tells of a friend of his who went to a large church to preach at a special Good Friday service. The weather was extremely bad and only a few people came. Apologetically, the host pastor said to the visiting pastor, "If it had not been for the bad weather, we would have had a large crowd to hear you tonight."

At first, it angered the visiting preacher, but quickly his anger turned to pity and contempt. Looking at his host, he said, "Do you realize what you have just said? If the weather had not been bad, a larger crowd would have come to this Good Friday service. Jesus died on Good Friday, but His followers did not come to the service because the weather was bad."[2]

Why don't Christians in our nation experience being reviled and persecuted, having all kinds of evil uttered against us falsely on Jesus' account? Is it because we are such a moral nation? No, we are not a terribly moral nation, if statistics about crime, violence, sexual behavior, drugs, environmental activity and the like is any measure. Perhaps Christians in America are not persecuted as they are in other places because we tend to be fairly lukewarm about what we believe. We do not usually take very big risks. And that itself is a big risk, because in the last book of the Bible, God speaks, saying, "I know your works: you are neither cold nor hot. Would that you were cold or hot! So, because you are lukewarm, and neither cold nor hot, I will spew you out of my mouth" (Revelation 3:15-16).

The Beatitudes end with the sure and certain promise that the result of keeping these Beatitudes will be persecution. It has been from the beginning. Tacitus, in his account of Nero's persecution about 65 A.D., tells of some of the things the first Christians faced: "Besides being put to death, they were made to serve as objects of amusement: they were clad in the hides of beasts and torn to death by dogs; others were crucified, others set on fire to serve to illuminate the darkness of the night."

The book *The Martyrdom of Polycarp* records that in 155 A.D., when Christian leader Polycarp was brought to the stadium, the Proconsul urged the old man to curse Christ, but Polycarp answered, "Eighty and six years have I served him, and he has done me no wrong; how then can I blaspheme my king, who saved me?" The

Proconsul threatened him with wild beasts and then with fire. Polycarp answered, "You threaten with the fire that burns for an hour and in a little while is quenched; for you do not know of the fire of the judgment to come, the fire of the eternal punishment, reserved for the ungodly. But why delay? Bring what you will."

"Blessed are those who are persecuted for righteousness sake, for theirs is the kingdom of heaven." It still happens to Christians in our time. Dr. Turner was the pastor of the American Church in Berlin before World War II. Once he visited Pastor and Mrs. Heinrich Niemoeller, the aged parents of Pastor Martin Niemoeller. Martin Niemoeller was a pastor who defied Hitler and spent many months in a concentration camp.

When the visit to Martin Niemoeller's parents was over, they stood at the door, talking. Dr. Turner said, "Grandmother Niemoeller held my left hand in her two hands. The grandfather of Martin's seven children patted my right hand and then put one hand on my shoulder. He said slowly, 'When you get back to America, do not let anyone pity the father and mother of Martin Niemoeller. Only pity any follower of Christ who does not know the joy that is set before those who endure the cross despising the shame. Yes, it is a terrible thing to have a son in a concentration camp. Paula here and I know that. But there would be something more terrible for us: if God had needed a faithful martyr, and our (son) Martin had been unwilling.' "[3]

Most of us would like to go through life loving and being loved. But of that goal, Jesus said, "Woe to you, when all speak well of you, for that is what their ancestors did to the false prophets" (Luke 6:26). And so Jesus made the peculiar observation that being harassed for the sake of your faith is a sign of God's favor.

People are not openly persecuted in this country for being Christian. It is more subtle. For example, in an academic setting, we can be free to discuss Sigmund Freud or Karl Marx, but try to have an open discussion of Christ and his teachings in a classroom in America and the discomfort will rise along with controversy. The "persecution" is subtle, and so we can drift away from our willingness to witness to what we believe.

Seated in a restaurant, no one will say you cannot bow your head to offer grace, but when was the last time you sat in a restaurant and bowed to offer grace before a meal? When I say a grace before a meal in a restaurant, I usually do it with my eyes open and my hands unfolded. Could we suffer from what we warn youth about — peer pressure?

Many of us work places where we have to show financial profit for our work. Seldom will someone say you cannot ask questions of ethics about how the money is made, but questions of Christian ethics usually remain in our mind without passing over our lips. *"Blessed* are you when men revile you and persecute you and utter all kinds of evil against you falsely on my account." But the threat of scorn from colleagues and reviling looks of peers hardly feels blessed.

Not only that, simply to suffer is not enough. As Augustine said, "The cause, not the pain, makes the martyr." Being injured for its own sake is not a virtue. There were times when Jesus was physically threatened but left to avoid being injured (Mark 8:27). When Jesus was praying in the Garden of Gethsemane knowing he faced the cross, he asked to be delivered from physical suffering: "Father, if it be possible, let this cup (of suffering) pass from me" (Matthew 26:39). Jesus accepted suffering when it was forced upon him, but he never sought or desired it.

When we try to be the best Christians we can, but find ourselves being reviled and persecuted, having all kinds of evil uttered against us falsely, we can say it is not fair, which it is not. If our concern is our immediate reward, we will pity ourselves for the injustice done us. However, if our concern is to do what we do for Jesus' sake, then the things that happen to us are seen in the larger context of these Beatitudes.

In fact, the normal and healthy response to being reviled and persecuted and having all kinds of evil spoken against us falsely is not gladness and joy. It is like the conversation between a parent and child at the checkout line at the grocery store. As the child considers the immediate delight of the candy displayed before him, the parent talks about how fortunate they are to have fresh spinach in their garden at home. We can hardly expect the child to be

69

overjoyed at the long-term health benefits of spinach while looking at the pleasure immediately available on the candy rack. That is why parents will spend time explaining this benefit and explaining it again and explaining it all over again.

It would be strange for a child to rush past the candy and potato chips to get to the health food section, though it would be wonderful. In the same way, it would be a strange and wonderful thing for people to find joy and gladness in the midst of persecution for the sake of their faith. But that has long been a unique characteristic of Christians. We are able to look through the words of this beatitude and understand the persecution in the light of God's will, and way through eternity, and the final promise that God's kingdom will come.

One night after the porch of his home was bombed, Martin Luther King wrote, "To our most bitter opponents we say ... 'Do to us what you will, and we shall continue to love you ... throw us in jail, and we shall still love you. Bomb our homes and threaten our children, and we shall still love you. Send your hooded perpetrators of violence into our communities at the midnight hour and beat us and leave us half dead, and we shall still love you ... one day we shall win freedom, but not only for ourselves. We shall so appeal to your hearts and conscience that we shall win you in the process, and our victory will be a double victory.' "[4]

The Beatitudes end with the sure and certain promise that we will receive the kingdom of heaven. We may have only a glimmer of it here and now, but most certainly we will see it fully hereafter. These beatitudes conclude by returning to the promise of the first beatitude, the promise that those who faithfully cling to these beatitudes will receive the kingdom of God.

"They who have endured much for what's right are God's people: they are citizens of His new Order. You all are God's people when others call you names, and harass you and tell all kinds of false tales on you just because you follow me. Be cheerful and good-humored, because your spiritual advantage is great. For that's the way they treated men of conscience in the past." (Jordon)

"Happy are those who are ridiculed for living their lives on a high spiritual plane. They are approved by God. Happy are those who are criticized and ridiculed and the subject of gossip because of their attempt to be Christlike. That ridicule has been heaped on others. Do not be disturbed about it, because God will give you a great reward." (*The Pulpit* 12/54)

"Blessed are those who are persecuted for righteousness' sake, for theirs is the kingdom of heaven. Blessed are you when men revile you and persecute you and utter all kinds of evil against you falsely on my account. Rejoice and be glad, for your reward is great in heaven, for so men persecuted the prophets who were before you." (RSV)

---

1. Neil Postman, *Amusing Ourselves To Death: Public Discourse in the Age of Show Business.*

2. *God's Psychiatry,* p. 157.

3. E.T. Thompson, *The Sermon On The Mount.*

4. Martin Luther King, Jr., *Strength To Love* (Harper and Row).

71